puppet

MURTAZA ALI

AURAQ

© 2020 Murtaza Ali

All rights reserved. No part of this publication may be reproduced, distributed, or transmitted in any form or by any means, including photocopying, recording, or other electronic or mechanical methods, without the prior written permission of the Publisher, Auraq Publications, except in the case of brief quotations embodied in critical reviews and certain other non-commercial uses permitted by copyright law.

Printed in the Islamic Republic of Pakistan.
Printed: September, 2020
Edition: 1st
ISBN: 978-969-749-014-1
Price: Rs 800 PKR, $08 US

ISLAMABAD, PAKISTAN

raabta@auraqpublications.com.pk | +92-300-0571-530
www.auraqpublications.com.pk | @AuraqPublications

A puppet isn't always made of threads and straws. Some are held through emotional bonds and played as well. The former's show could last for an hour or so. But, the later has to obey the cautions till the master finds a new one.

Let the show begin.

THOUGH, I DON'T WANT TO

My mother wakes me up in the morning

I wake up with half lids open

Desire to join the rest slumber, but

She flurries me for the bus stop

Though, I don't want to

Life wants me to gear up

For the challenges, for the barricades

Might pop out, in the time to come

I'd have to deal with them

Though, I don't want to

I aboard on the bus

Don't know where the way leads to

Only I know,

It would drop me to the varsity

Though, I don't want to

PUPPET

Wonder to see the kids on roadway

Happy on entering to Erudition

If they can, why couldn't I?

Pondering on this, move into the varsity

Though, I don't want to

SHE

I rose

She pulled me down

I barged ahead

She put barricades after barricades

I smiled

She hit me in face

I gathered flowers around

She replaced it with thorns

I bought balloons

She brought needles into action

I swam at large

She urged sharks after me

I kept myself motivated

She kept herself vicious

I tried it fill my cycle with Jasmine

She succeeded in filling it with regrets

I couldn't win over her

Since, she is my life

IS IT FINE?

I cannot exceed

My count from 99

And reach to my end – 100.

I get it.

Fate doesn't allow it.

I invoke the Lord's blessings

Each time as ordained.

I follow all His decrees

Maybe not all,

As I am a weak creation – human

Nevertheless, I don't get the blessings I invoke.

I get it.

Fate doesn't allow it.

Life used to be so good

So satiating, so fresh

The only headache I had

The school, and

Not getting my favourite meal at lunch

Rest, life was jolly and honey – sweet.

Unlike now, where every breath

Pinches me hard and though I can't

But I must inhale it.

Life doesn't value my choices anymore.

I get it.

Fate doesn't allow it.

I am away from debauchery, and

Being coquette

As it is not permissible, and

Rewards are promised for those

Who abstain their selves

Unlikely, those who practise it

Will get whipped.

But every then and now

I encounter virility

I must go through dissoluteness

I get mocked of my chastity

I am getting these rewards instead

Of what's promised.

I get it

Fate doesn't allow it.

The day will come when your prayers be answered, you will feel light as never before, all the unanswered questions in your heart will subside, there won't be anymore regrets for the choices you made, you will have the time of your life. You just need to be patient. Death is near. You will get rid of all these nuisances.

THE SAME HE

The journey has been tiringly long

The driver, fate, is still keen

To the damnation of his spirit -

Long lost the battle and

Surrendered to the cause of fate.

At a crossroad, he tries to escape the bond,

Loosened at the other end

As of now,

That loop holds someone else.

But the promises that everyone took

Manipulation of words, were echoed

From heart and his soul, and those promises

Made him prefer his damnation over parting ways

From what he names his "life", as

How could one be alive without life?

As the journey continues,

He is being mocked of his foolishness

As he embraced his damnation, rather

The other way

Which could have set him free from the shackless of

Dejection and nympholepsy.

But he doesn't defy any, as he knows

None of the mockers have carried out

This sweet - bitterness in their heart ever

And, he himself chose his damnation

Because, he yearns for it more than ever, as

How could one be alive without life?

So, the mockers are to be given no heed.

The journey gets tens and now

The "life" gives a stern remark

He didn't do anything to save

The other end of bond from

Slipping into someone else's hand.

Better he knows, he begged mercy

But it didn't come from heaven.

Neither wholly nor partially

His prayers were listened.

But he can't retort to life with this

As, the life might get drive away from him

And then, how could one be alive without life?

Life asks him to pluck flowers for her

He does so but life finds them of unpleasing fragrance

It is because he is changed now, life scorns.

Better he knows, he plucked the flowers

With same delicacy and present it with same love

As he used to do back then.

Maybe, as of now, her heart is inclined towards the one

Who is holding the other end of the bond, and

It makes her nose and eyes unable to catch the love

Wrapped in those flowers, he plucked for her.

He is satisfied with her remarks,

As if he discussed the possibility

Life might get away from him, and

How could one be alive without life?

He has no concern for her now,

Life makes this remark with great disdain.

Better he knows, he is baffled in boundaries

Drawn between him and her

Only it makes him to say a thousand words

Or to say nothing at times.

But he cannot assure her that it's all for her sake

As life might get away, and

How could one be alive without life?

Meanwhile, the journey halts for a while

The life has the reminiscences of time

When the life belonged to him, only

But these reminiscences brought wrath on her side and

She hates him, as he is happy to see her cry, and

He has bowed to the fate's justice.

He is willing to part ways, and

The journey till now, and

His kneeling to hers every word

Was just for fun and without any hearty emotion.

He is changed now.

Better he knows, he has cried

Throughout the journey.

He has cursed fate and its decrees

On every bump in the journey.

His heart is still filled with love for her,

He is still fond of her embrace,

He still belongs to her,

But she doesn't.

But he cannot retort with this,

As the life might get away, and

How could one be alive without life?

WORDS

Driven by handful of sweet memories

I implored for an instance.

Little I knew,

The ears are not mine, and

The words can lose their worth,

At times and over time.

THE OLD ME

The old me

Never thought of the thorns

The rose accompanied, and

Just lived the beauty

I could behold.

The old me

Never got out of happy endings

Following a topsy-turvy journey, and

Believed in the mirthful experience

Of love and romance.

The old me

Never considered true

The tragedies I heard, and

Had faith in His bounties

For His creation.

Oppositely, now I realize

Rose is incomplete without its thorns

Love is not bound to end in happiness

And He is not just the greatest well wisher

But the greatest judge of our actions too.

BECAUSE I NEED YOU

U remember the million mistakes

I committed in my hard times

Nor the love, fate bonded us with

Hereby, I want to remind you

Time to hate is gone

Come back, because I need you

Peep into the past

Witness the moments of love we had

When we felt lucky to have each other

I used to your hobby, and

So were you to me

Hug me tight, because I need you

Today, my apologies seem disloyal

But it was you

Who believed in mistakes and not in love.

Nevertheless, I beseech you

Let us start the voyage of love – again

Because I need you

Accept your defeat. Accept that you have been dumped. Accept that you have been deceived. Accept that you have been lied to. There is no shame in accepting that you failed. But, if you keep living in fool's paradise, your life will get shallow day by day and one day you will fall down as a minaret falls due to rotten foundations. You are same as the minaret because you too overlooked your weaknesses and considered yourself grand while you weren't. Your heart wanted to feel the pangs of loss, but you forced it into pretensions. Once, you come out of such whims, only then you will be able to become grand in real means.

THE NORTH STAR

(1)

Once, Two Swans

Set out for a new beginning,

A journey to cover,

A destination to reach,

Pledges to regard, errors to forsake.

Amidst the waters,

Among the waves

Swans knocked at a tempest

Too strong, too overwhelming

For Swans to remain – one soul.

The tempest took its supper

The love sliced; the affections divided

The bonds relinquished.

(2)

The parted Swan

In Waters – gloomy and sorrow.

Living the death,

Paddling in despair and

Invoking a refuge,

Lost, almost lost the fortitude

Against the rude and rampant waters.

But, a sparkle met his vision

It was a star

It was the Star.

It lifted his hopes, fortified his wings,

Against the waters,

Against the rude and rampant waters.

(3)

The rejuvenated Swan

Once lost, now, restored Swan

Set out for a new beginning

Under the Star, Along the Star.

The love was lovelier than ever

The bond was stronger than ever

Seemed that of souls

Nor of Paths.

For accompanying each other

The voyage pursued and prolonged

In love, regard and care

The rude and rampant waters

Turned into cozy and calm ones.

(4)

They met in a night

Complemented each other

In Nights.

But, the nights faded and

The disillusionment started

For the Swan,

For the parted, rejuvenated Swan.

Nights vanished and took the Star along with.

Is Star only meant for nights?

Was it a Star?

Or just another rude and rampant wave?

Swan reflected and took by waters.

Unlike the star, for an eternal company.

FATE

You would have listened, read and observed various implications of fate. Some say that it's a pre-written pathway of your life. Others put it like a cage where one is entrapped. One may state that it is nothing but just a set of excuses one brings forth upon failure. Succinctly, each one in your surrounding will give his experience of life and nothing more, considering fate. So, shall I dare to put forward mine? Would the sick fate allow me to do so? Or, she is going to instil itching in my fingers at the right moment; my fingers would shrink and go paralyzed with my brain stop processing! Wait! Oh! She is clement meanwhile. I didn't get a stroke or developed a tumour while daring to denounce the decrees of the malevolent fate. No one exactly knows the tenure of the gentle cycle of fate so let me get straight to the point. Fate, I don't want to waste any of my efforts indicting it. Because, she is so wicked that my assault won't pacify its aggression, let alone my cries. Well, fate is nothing but a hand, a helping hand. Yes! a helping humane hand. Fate firstly knock you down with a blow so strong that you get buried alive. Subsequently, you will start pushing hard for your release. You will cry. You will yell (Trust me you cannot do anything else in true). Or, some put a hard shell over them and portray as nothing happened. But, deep down they are shaken. A long gloomy span will pass and then you will feel a guidance towards a brighter pathway. Success will seem at hand to you. Everything will start seeming pleasant to you. Though, at first you think that it's better to live in dark as you are used to it now. But glitters always dupe man. So, you shun everything and proceed. As you consider everything good coming towards you as a reward for your suffering and cries (obviously heard this fairy tale once in life). You start getting to the top, step by step. You achieve first goal, then second, then third, followed by another slap by fate which again buried you alive. The cycle continues and man gets deceived by the fate and goes underground. Fate is all. Sorry, fate is not all. Fate is a ....

CHOICES

We live

Wholly on choices

Sometimes, ours

Rest; others

Ours can be right

Ours can be wrong

But, a choice once made

Can't be revert.

It never see whose it was,

Ours or others',

Is no consideration for her,

Only thing it registers

Is life, only of ours

My life seems,

Right, Up to the mark

To rest of the world

Applauses, praises

Tributes, admirations

I acknowledged - whole life.

But, I and

Only I know

Deep down my heart

The life was neither right

Nor wrong.

Rather it was just choices, I made

Or made to make.

Being cursed is nothing but making wrong decisions that subsequently ruin your life.

RESTORATION

It was all so romantically calm

We enjoyed every bliss of love

Though, we had hard times

But the lives soon got restored

I guess, somewhere in the mid of

Such a restoration, he raced a little further

Leaving me behind entangled

In the cycles of memories, and

His love I couldn't achieved

To live and wishes a restoration

On his part again

Where it is impossible.

I NEED NO MORE HOPES

For now, I am destroyed

Yet there glimmers something,

The ray of hope

Though, it seems promising

A new turn in my life

That could possibly lead

To the heights

I dreamt and worked for

But how could I possibly trust it

As all the prior castles were doomed

As I step onto their stones.

This may also aid

To the turmoil I am into already

HAPPY BIRTHDAY

Stars bowed

Flowers wilted

Colors faded

Spring receded

All enticements couldn't endure that of you,

You accessioned to the throne of beauty.

The day you came:

Enchanted whole land

With your admiring aura

Being cheerful,

And prodigiously Majestic

Captivated each

Charmer, known before you.

The day is again here

Throne of yours

Is yet to be inlaid by another gem

So, keep enjoying your reign

With Best Wishes

And Heaps, that of blessings.

I am pleased

To greet an Angelica

A Happy Birthday...

HAPPY BIRTHDAY?

So, the day is here again, and

The majesty will come down

From her throne.

The throne is carved over with

The beauty no beholder can behold,

The charm no wizard can invoke,

Enticement no human can refuse.

She came down to cherish her moment

To relish the progression of her life, and

To cherish the happening with her disciples.

As she believes,

The elation will last forever, and

The petals will increase in number

Amplifying the spread of fragrance

To quest the need of her disciples.

But the boon had to end, and

Her smile had to fade

As, this time petals didn't increase

Rather, the thorns took their charge

Making the most happening occasion

The site of forever loss for her

As she is handed over to another stalk

To hold and to raise her

Though, her stature is emboldened now

As the stalk is more lasting, and

Bolder of its predecessor

Nevertheless, she won't be the only one on throne now

As she owns a share nor the whole of it

Which make her miss the nascent stalk

And lament her own birthday

The happy birthday?

I DON'T KNOW

I dared to inquire

What is it?

That pinches her,

Making her shut.

Every comfort we enjoyed once.

She just responds, every time:

"I Don't know"

She encaged herself

In a morbid castle

Imbued with gloom and forlorn.

I climb to the window

Through the bridge of her hair and ask.

Can I liberate you into a land of bloom and glee?

She just responds, every time:

"I Don't know"

She: How do I look

I: Not mine

FORSAKEN

You are the minaret

Entombing the beauty underneath

Making the world void of it

Each beholder desires,

Knitting their oblivion,

A taste of the beauty you hold

The beholders must be told

The sacrifices of the forsaken soul

To cement the tomb and

Burry the heart embracing a heart

It held once.

PUPPET

Released myself from all the ties

In seek of some free air

Where I could live on my own

Where I could die on my own

But, the world isn't a favorable place to live alone

We need someone to live by our side

The someone, who embraces us

Even if we stink of failures,

Even if we are not an epitome of grace and virtue, and

Even if we are doomed

Owing to our own doings

The someone will imbibe the whole of us into her life.

Soon, I found the someone

Who promised to live by my side

Who pledged to let me live in herself

The voyage started and progressed pleasantly

But, soon, new threads and ropes came into play

And, I am tied again

To fulfill someone's indications, and

I remain a puppet

You lament that you have seen soaring waves. But, someone else out there has rode them and might still be riding them.

THE DAY WE MET

A fair morning

U came down the street,

Taking little steps

Your waving hairs,

Exalting you to an angelica

Your blinking brown eyes

Pierced into my heart

Left no life in me

And so your haughty eyebrows

And so your symmetrical lips

U passed by me

Smiling and chattering

Made me give up on you

Alluring My heart, my senses

I became a captive of your aroma

Considering the day we met

YOU – MINE

Remember the day?

We met

In the love garden

Where flowers were your looks

Petals, your lips

Buds, your blinking eyes

We got surrounded

By warmth of each's love

Remember the glances?

We casted

Upon each other

Made me, give up on you

Bond Soul, mine with yours

Accept, being captive

Of Your Supremacy,

Since then I've been yours

And You - Mine.

COME FLY WITH ME

Come, hold my hand

Accompany me in this journey

Shun all your routines

Give up on all your attentions

For I have dreamt a better world for you

Just put your belief in me, and

My love for you.

I will make you ride waves of fate

Which otherwise dominate us

I will make you sit atop tempests, and

All its whirls will be under your say

I will make you soar to heavens

Where you truly belong

Unlikely to this grief stricken humanly land

You need not to follow your dreams

Your dreams will follow you

You just, come fly with me

Their story would have a sad or happy ending. But ours, just won't end.

A COFFEE MUG

One could grasp the mug from anywhere

But, for me,

I will hold it from right there

Where you would sneakily tickle

My fingers with your nails

When no waiter had focus on us.

Though, you have changed

The person to tickle

But I take coffee even today

Just to feel the same tickle and

To sense your presence around

As it is the only way

To stay alive.

You remember

How I used to get lost

In glimpse of you

Sipping the coffee off your mug

The site of your lips

Getting foamed over those sips

Witnessing the foam on your lips

Was always more than

Embracing yours with mine.

Today, I take the sips

Filling the emptiness in me

With the reminisces and

Embracing the brim of the Mug

You once gifted me on birthday

With the same passion and devotion

As if, I am embracing your revered lips

With mine.

THE LAST KISS

It drew closer

Receding the gaps, and

Fostering new bonds between us.

The veins concentrated; all, in chest

I, failed to match the passion in those eyes,

Reclined effortless and opened the doors

Imploring those arms to embrace me.

As, it is the only (favourable) end to the parable,

The only solution to the all the Apollo's riddles,

The only shelter to a vagabond,

The final straw a sparrow brought,

That evening, to fortify her nest,

The answer to all my prayers.

Stoned at hearing beats of that heart,

As the bodies merged,

Lost the count of mine.

The warmth that breath had

Made me short of mine.

My lips, upon peck of those steamy lips

Turned into a desolate land,

In want, to quench the thirst,

I let my lips burn in the blazes.

Eventually, we became one, and

My beatings stopped.

I am yet to apprehend

Whether, it drew out my life, or

Infused it's in my body.

Was it the kiss of life, or

That of death?

Well, I still exist (maybe)

Somewhere, over the lines of those petals,

(Maybe not) and have been brushed away,

By some more delicate strokes.

TO THE QUEEN I ONCE SERVED

The breeze never come alone

You know what does it bring along?

It brings memories and the past,

We spent together.

The happy and satiating past

We lived,

When you weren't someone's princess

Rather, my queen.

As the breeze blew

A moment ago,

It flashed open my windows, and

The curtains split,

Setting the spectacle

It seems, as if

The wind has carried my vision

Again, to the fairyland

Which is not so far

But, just right after the windows

As the curtains and windows stay blow – open

I witness, I and you

Enjoying Pistachio flavoured Ice-cream at a Parlour,

Where you refuse to have more

Being concerned of your growing weight

But I put the scoop on your tongue

For you to gulp it down

As I love my chubby queen.

And the wind gets harsh

Clearing my vision more to the site

When I pick up the tissue

To remove the cream

Off your lips and

You take the tissue of my hand

And blessed it with your lipstick mark

So, the queen is remembered forever

In my wallet.

I may have lived my fluctuating part in your life, but you will enjoy your undiminishing status in mine forever.

You are not a secret to be hidden. You are my pride to be boastful about.

NOTHING, THE SAME ANYMORE

We think

Everything, everyone, would stay

We'd receive the same love, the same care,

We have everything.

But,

Fantasies last a little

Till they are crushed, and

We fail to realize how

Our fellow beings, family,

Elders as well as younger ones

Can give us a back seat

Can divert their paths

Ignore, and don't care about us.

We, the same as used to be

They, maybe not the ones

As ever.

No, I think,

No, they are the same

The ones, who loved us

We, being their priority,

Enjoyed the bliss

But,

If they are the same, then

It's, I reckon the cruel

Time, which is changed...

I LOVE YOU

I love you! I just can't live without it! I haven't seen anyone like you! You know what! I feel really special to have you. I kinda feel real with you. I don't have to feign and it's just the true me with you. I forgot to mention the most "adorable" one, "Thankyou for entering into my life sweetheart." You would have certainly felt relatable to most of them. Maybe, you have used them as well (not being judgemental). It is only due to the fact we are living in an "I love you generation." We all admittedly find all of these phrases odd, cringy, and any other eww adjectives you want to add along. But the time we get into a relationship, we cannot live without these words. Sometimes, we actually demand such words which could led us to the Barbie world and a relation might not get last longer if these "adorable" efforts are not put into.

Let's first state why we fall into the trap of love and why, like why the heck our generations are getting into it day by day in an exponential manner (even when they can't write all such "adorable" phrases). To be honest, our media is playing an "adorable" role in it. Though it has multiple other functions to perform but the least it does is expose an "adorable" child or a teenager to notions of "Ishq" "Pyar" "Muhabbat" and recently the words like "BAE" have also been inculcated in their minds. (Damn! I miss my grade 6th crush. I just had the word "Mine" to call her. Wish I had word like "Bae". Its classy. Children now a days have so much at their disposal) So, what happens the notions are locked in their minds and we all know how much dedicated we are towards each other in our families are now a days. The overlooking by parents leads to children feeling lacking something. It could be lack of care, lack of confidence boosters, lack of talking. I will only address the most common "lacks". Subsequently, the "adorable" children fill the deficiency by approaching to the opposite gender and it is a fact hormone do come into play. In short, the "I Love You" generation is suffering from a disease known as "I am yours and you are ONLY mine." Let's address a bonus issue. Why can't we forget the past so easily or what is the issue of "Pehla Nasha, Pehla Khummar." John Locke, a philosopher said that our minds are blank slate. Anything gets written on it with the passage of life becomes our experience or rules for future processing. (Trust me it is the easiest version of any philosophical notion you would ever witness). Considering this, once we get anything written on our "adorable" portion of "love" on the slate for the first time. It would be there now and is added as an experience, as a rule for future. We all know that removing anything from a slate takes an effort and even if the slate is clean of the prior writing, yet it isn't like the new one which didn't have anything written. Humans are the same. The slates once incorporate anything, it becomes hard to remove it and even if another incorporation takes place. It isn't like the "Pehla Nasha, Pehla Khumaar."

Note: The word "adorable" has been used as a scapegoat for any slang you can think of and all the information provided is inspired by around 10 slates.

THE RAIN DROP

An ember caught a flame and

A Phoenix rose, in a desert,

Amongst the vultures.

Solely, confronted the red beaks,

Bruised and seared into his own fire

In the hands of the red beak avians

But, never settled for being subjected.

He grew with all the bruises and stigmas

Over his self, around his self, and

One day, he overwhelmed the vultures

All the red beaks left, and he remained

The sole survivor,

With all his integrity and composure restored.

But the desert started haunting him, soon

The loneliness started getting better of him

All the fire he has inside,

Started burning him within.

He looked up to the sky

To the wandering cloud,

His only love and companion throughout his life, and

Asked for some mercy, some miracle

Some miraculous rain drops in the desert

To quench his thirst of an eternal companionship

Not like that of a wanderer cloud

Or that of evil red beaks

Rather, a companionship which could lead him

To equanimity within.

The cloud didn't answer, and the nights approached

The nights came as a season never ending.

He saw his imminent end, and that too

Through his own fire.

Meanwhile, within the night

A miracle fell from the sky on him

A drop as sharp as it pierced through his fire-body, and

Reached his heart, enveloped his heart.

As he slowly succumbed

To the cool warmth of that miraculous companion

The vultures started approaching, again, and

Again, the bout started.

But they can't overcome the Phoenix now

As, he has attained the powers of all powers,

The love of his life, and

Soon, the cooled Phoenix vanquish the evils.

Since then, the fire never lit

Nor any desert remained dry.

May the birds of the forthcoming spring never experience the autumn passed.

I YIELD!

To all the daunting blue shades:

I yield!

I'll no longer withstand – nor be able to,

The odds, the tempests

Brought into the contest with me.

Where could it all have had maneuvered best

Than in the hands of the (only) enemy,

The sapient and sneering – fate.

Since long,

The same agent had been despising

Mankind's desires and designs

It doesn't give heed to the strife,

Nor the labor he puts,

To beget a dream, an endeavor.

All the bounties bestowed,

Each honorific attained,

The love and confidants, one meets,

The unsavory fate scorns all.

The hard tiles of splendor and (earnt) glory

One treads become

Inferno; kindled by jilts and deceptions.

The blazes of the inferno,

Can sear through any valor, any grandeur,

As it is curated by malignant fate.

Eventually, one yields all his-selves.

I, too, did not enjoy any prerogative, and

Pulled down from the zenith

To the pits of forlorn.

THE PUPPETS OF REMORSE

One longs for other

Other – another

Speculates intrigues,

Forsakes pledges.

Owe: subsides affinities

Strangles the desires – incorporeal

Spurns; threads – soul.

Presumption:

Love, obsessive thoughts,

A vain endeavour, Overrides each.

Each to each

Malign, each and each:

Existence, concerns, empathy.

Stigmatizes, Incarnate blemishes

To the lofty wild soul.

Protracts the splits

Venerates the momentary over

That is ardent and elevated, romance.

Passes the course

Being astray.

Misses the privileges, of

Pure, soulful sentiments.

Eventually mourns,

Each to each,

Over the choices,

Not to be made.

And grace the garden with

Regret, and only remorse.

I WILL GET HEALED

With all the bruises and aches

I will get healed one day

No matter how penetrating your lies are

I will get healed one day

Though, you forgot to look back

To the stage you left me to act upon

Yet, I will get healed one day

Thoughts do strike me to quit but I don't

Because, I know, I will get healed one day

Whether you make me re-live or

Keep me in the dark dungeons of past

I will get healed anyway

Even if you don't care and

Won't live to see the restored me

Yet, I will get healed one day.

Let yourself heal. I must tell you it won't be a peaceful process. There would be surging waves, tempests, destruction. You may quit and let yourself sway in the horrid darkness. But it's the destructed portion where re-construction occurs. You can't just build another wall over an already existing wall. So, don't panic while losing it all. Let the time take everything you own. Let it burn you. Let it pierce all the ills into you. You will restore your being, eventually. That's how it works. That's what they call life.

A DREAM LIFE

Last Night

Found it tough to sleep

But, a dream waited for me there.

It was fragrant and flowery-

The mirage of a dream life,

Overwhelming and burning deep

Blithesome, Wondrous and Ineffable

Sightly existence of the Angelica

Felt ecstatic

Being with the Angelica.

Allured me deep

As Fanny did to Keats

But the journey lasted a little

Same as Anne and Byron's.

Again, I am in my world

Arena of grief and despair

MURTAZA ALI

THE MOONWALK

I yearn,

Looking to the moon,

Be at your side, once

In my life,

Our fingers entwined,

Our shoulders brushed,

Your hair dusting my shoulder.

Following the steps,

Our hearts lead us on to

In these downtown's alleys

With breeze hitting us cold.

These stones under our feet

Seem the grey of the moon,

And the walk feels a walk on moon.

As the company I would have is itself,

Of the Moon.

Even if one's world is of smoke and glass, he could still want you to be beside him in that fantasy, make him feel just a little good. You may not know what drove him to that fantasy but the one that stands by him in those fantasies will do matter in the end.

JUST A LITTLE MORE

The time has come

The ship has honked

The navigation is checked

The inventory is all stacked up

It is you to depart.

The winds just gave a hint,

They would stay strong

And guide the ship

Straight away, from me,

Towards the spooky yet elegant Castles,

The castles where a gallant awaits

To put the Queen's crown

On the princess I behold, meanwhile.

Hereby, I wish to

Catch your angelic impressions,

Bless myself with your embrace,

Create heavens around

With your presence beside me,

Just a little more

Call you mine,

Just a little more,

Love you as mine,

Just a little more.

DEBACLE OF ANOTHER MIRAGE

I found someone

As she is me, or

I am her

Same personas, perceptions, sentiments

Residing in that soul.

That soul claimed,

A lost half: that's to mine.

Both halves have

Wandered for culmination

Only possibility to make it happen,

The search for the left over half shall be completed.

Eventually, destiny relented

And both halves unified.

We embarked on a differed tale

Shun the past,

Blurred or highlighted instances

We have been through

As both souls have yearned

For each other since long.

Now, the chasms within souls

Started to fill with:

Affections, intimacy, love

And both experienced

The warmth of completion

They longed for.

The journey started and stayed

Cozy and clear ahead

Everything seemed a reward

Of the piercing thorns

Each soul endured.

No one was now skeptical

Of this romantic progression

Love being the Star

To guide and usher us

To the dreamt world.

With no questions, complaints, regrets left

Both of us felt grateful

Over this culmination.

But, only to my presumption

The other half soon pronounced

Me as not what she desired, or

Not the admirable enough version of mine

That could stimulate her love, and

She was illusioned, or

Needed a carriage for her escape

That I provided with a bond

Of love and servitude of soul

To the other soul.

O' How well you extracted the sap off me , that the autumn felt mirthful of itself.

THE LIFE SPENT

The bud of my life

Never given a chance to bloom

As plucked before my full glory

Destined me to be deprived

Of sunshine, of butterflies

I desired to spread:

The fragrance, the happiness, the joy

But, now my stalk could only offer:

The thorns, the pain, the harm

Though, dewdrops might wash their anguish

Those, aggrieved of me

The drops would turn their morale

As glittery as the diamonds

Wish, my grieves have been too

Wiped with a flow:

A flow of her love, her allure, her enticement

But, wishes are waves

Touch for a while and leave the shore

And these waves left me

With an eternal affliction

Of destitute, of condemnation

And transfixed me to a life of

A withered grass of a sunken lake,

A sail of wrecked ship,

A marble of a demolished fort.

I have lived a life

Where fate didn't know

How to compose, what to write

That's what I'd say

When I'll glance over

The Life spent

Life is a test. We all know this. We have been taught this. But, what this test really is? Is it the test of our deeds? Is it the test of blind following? Is it the test of not getting astray? Is it the test of our choices? Or, it's just the test of living in peace with the capricious calamities we get exposed to.

THE LIFE NOT SPENT

There are no dark clouds

No heavy showers of rain

The sky is bright to its fullest

As the Sun has overpowered

The daunting dark clouds of fate

Everything seems happy now inside out

I am not staggering rather striding towards my goals

The pleasant blows of wind push me ahead

Likewise, a balloon appears

In the brightest sky from nowhere

Encouraging and motivating me

Inciting a fire inside

The fire, that is not going to burn me

As all the fires from the past has done,

Collapsed my Kingdom,

Turned me into ashes,

Ashes, trodden by the regrets, afterwards

Rather, the balloon seems saying to me

"O Adonis Lad!

Why do you cling to the wind at the back?

Clinging to everything past you has no worth

Than to push you forward.

You are only meant to ride it, as I do

You will keep rising riding the past winds, as I do

You will, for sure, excel, and

Everything, you will find beneath you

Which you were once clung to

Just keep rising, don't look behind.

May the balloon always hover over me.

If life has a race why this race doesn't have any finish line? If it is said to be a spectacle why don't the curtains close till the next act?

Love is just like a candle. It will give you light and warmth in your life but in the end you would only find yourself grounded.

GOD AND HER

I hear a distant call

So soulful and mortifying

Is it the God's call?

Wait! He is not appeased

Owing to my ignorance

Towards His decrees.

Is it You?

But likewise Him

You are not mine.

Both held me tight

With their rope of love

Whenever, I tried to set loose myself

Even a little, and do something

I; my instincts aspired

The loop was tightened even more.

Eventually, they set me loose

After eating the bulk of me.

Then, what is it

If it is not who created me

Nor, who I created of my love.

Pulling me somewhere,

I don't know where; nowhere.

Is it my piece of love?

That you promised to give

But acted Him and left me

To wonder at my life

Till eyes to meet Him.

SURVIVAL

What do you know about survival? Obviously, you would have heard and read plenty of survivals, from a highly romantic Prince, born with miserable accounts of life stridden through all the vicissitudes and eventually becoming an acclaimed Prince after fighting a duel with the malevolent Governor of the incumbent King, to a more realistic happening considering a dilapidated fortune turning into of billions only through hard work, resilience and patience. But I am not going to talk about the cliché patterns. I am not going to say anything about the result of a survival. I would just narrate my theory about me surviving. I don't know it may also turn a blunder and make me a ridiculous piece on earth. Do focus on the use of language as I am using "may" not "might", implying that there is a likely possibility of failure. Before surviving I must tell you that what hit me that I realized the importance of the word "survival".

Life is going at its normal and peaceful pace. I had the love of my life in me, supporting, caring and loving me like I have never experienced. I have been getting accolades after accolades and recognition after recognition. Despite of all the appreciations, I didn't get pompous of my art and still tried to excel in it. Suddenly, life bumped into a rock whilst the journey. I fumbled but recovered soon. But the road ahead never got the same plain road and the road now was only of bumps. I started losing hold on my love, career, education, friends and life, one after the other. A healing point come in way. I took a sigh of relief and prayed that my all hardships shall end here and as I come out of this healing point I starts rising again as I was once on my way up to the skies. Unfortunately, the healing point injected more negativity in me, and I didn't get well after passing the point. Once again, the road got difficult to cross with no way back. I kept on creeping to make it to the end and the journey is still due with I am having no one closed to pet my back to say "Yeah! you got all what it takes" and the journey is still due. You will surely be wondering what my take on survival is. Well, I would say that just let the road to your end hurt you the best it could. Let its thorns get inject in your skin. Give it to the very last drop of blood you got in your veins. If you have been exposed to such road by fate than just accept the fact that you are doomed. Don't indulge yourself in far-fetched ideals. You won't recover if you get romantic themes of staying positive, motivating yourself all the time, it would all end once and for all, in your head. Facing your damnation with open eyes is much better and helpful than staying positive. Just keep limping, creeping whatsoever you can but just don't stop. That's the key. Get yourself hurt and wounded but just don't stop. Just don't stop. I repeat just don't stop.

LET ME BE MYSELF

I am done

I am done with your allures

I am done with your embraces

As I am not the shark

Who want to prey on your curves

But the one wanting

A soul to get unified to.

Now, I don't want any of your lies

I want to live with the truth

Even if it is hurting

It will be the real you

I am not only to quench your desires, and

To make you feel over the moon

I am to exist; I am to be known

As, others are.

If you are not into this

Then, I am tired

I am tired living a Phantom

A riddle so allusive to me,

Even though, it considers me.

Give me my life

Pull me out of the shroud, and

Let me know,

Let yourself know,

Let everyone know:

I am a human with a real existence, and

Not just a vantage point,

Belonging only to you.

FUTURE

As Greek antiquities to wisdom

Nature is to Beauty,

So are eyes to life.

I close my eyes,

Because, pause and rest,

All I need.

Contrary, I envisioned,

Future: the time yet to come

Is intimidated, overwhelmed,

Trodden and eroded.

As the haunting memories

Still dwell.

I wonder

How would I get rid of?

The memories, the aches

They ask me to shun the past and look into my future. But I don't see anything. I just witness a void space filled of nothing but darkness, vehement frustration and despair. Even if there comes anything pleasant, it won't do any good. As, there won't be "YOU" holding my hand and patting my shoulder to affirm that "I am the best man ever lived." So, it all comes to no future without you and just a chain of events leading to my end.

THE LITTLE DAMSEL

In the blue waters,

There sailed a little bewitcher,

Paddling along the bold waves,

The Little damsel.

The epitome of beauty and valor

Seemed, a sightly vale

With hair as dark cataract

Eyes, the shooting stars,

That can make any swan,

Deserted or accompanied,

Long to paddle in those ponds.

Or, she is, just, an escape

Which poesy has led the gallant to.

Baffled and confounded,

He pondered.

Nay, she isn't a nightingale,

Nor, it is an escape away from,

"Where Beauty cannot keep her lustrous eyes"

Soon, the wind drew him closed

To that inexplicable scene.

The shimmering symmetry

Of the sailor there,

Brought not only him; rather

Several sharks visited the sight.

The grey and black sharks

Wanted to prey on her curvaceous body.

But, unlike the sharks

The passions were sacred for him

Neither the curves, nor the gleams

Overcome the humane gallant's capacity

To repress the aroused animal thirsts.

As peace can't be sustained

Where two opposites meet.

Hence, in a while,

There wrangled profanity and purity.

His belief - Spirituality overrides physical desires

Made him presuppose,

The staggering him will get an air of gaiety.

But, none of the warring parties

Can vanquish the tides of fate.

No matter, how wicked or sacred one is,

Fate presides over all, and

The damsel rides; made to ride, the tides.

Sharks vanished, as the savory treat was gone.

But two nympholepts: sea and gallant,

Were doomed to only wonder,

Would there be any return of damsel?

Or, they will remain as maudlin; with

The fate domineering all.

IS SHE THIS? IS SHE THAT?

Is she a riddle?

Only Apollo could solve.

Or an escape, the great Lake,

Keats aspires to get on.

Or is she the spirit,

Wordsworth perceives among woods.

I reckon,

She is my nympholepsy.

Why won't she be!

As she is more to me

Than Layla is to Qais.

Yet, all these are just conjectures

And the conjectures aren't worthy of her name.

As: she is a faith to follow,

The thrust of waters -

Keeping the ships afloat, and

The dance of a Sufi

While, meeting his beloved.

Seemingly, I ought to offer

The same devotion

To be one with her.

You resemble my each loss – an underachievement

THE CIRCLES OF FATE

I got pierced,

I got stabbed,

I got jilted.

But I had no answer

To each and all – assaults.

Nor do anyone believed

Anyone could receive so much

Marks in the hands of the merciful.

Added: "Man, the most beloved creature"

Surely, the dissents were apt

As, I have nothing on my body

Whilst, the capacity of man

Lingers only on appearance,

And, too keen to notice

The turmoil within,

Orchestrated by the same merciful.

Yet, I believe there is nothing

To contempt for in the dissidents

It's her forte to dupe innocent man

Making them blind to see

The circles around one's eyes,

The circles of fate.

THE LAST SLEEP

Ah, the sweet fragrance

Your hair bears

Resounds with the Heavens.

As, I heard,

There are milky canals

Likewise, your cheeks;

Fresh scented fruits,

Like the taste of your lips.

I have wondered till now

What's the symbol of the cataracts?

I heard of, in Heavens, in this world.

As now I lean under your shade

The dark brown hair,

Make me realize

There isn't any possible symbol of heavens.

It's just the heavens itself,

Under which I want to sleep now

A sleep that is not destined to waking up, and

A sleep that ends me - with you.

INTO THE DEADLAND

The touch didn't bring

The cheeks and bones

It lingered upon before.

The glossy lips

Felt like only I

Own that gloss.

The eyes I behold

Seemed, have only I

In the lens.

The cataract of hair over me

Made me assert

Only I have laid down under it.

The love and beloved

All and all felt

As if I am the only one

At the receiving end

The romance was delightful

The meeting was tranquilizing

The encounter was satiating

But only once,

She was laying flowers at my grave

And I was into the deadland.

Darkness: When you look into your life from now to onwards and you don't find anyone beside you, with all your miseries growing and your steadfastness lessening.

THE HUNTER AND THE HUNTED

Among the vicissitudes

Two swans lived - happily

One – too caring,

The other – heavenly beautiful.

Both the lives were a life.

The life others envied.

As they could offer nothing more

Because, love can fight each and all

Malevolent designs, indeed.

Indeed? That too each and all designs?

The known fallacy is busted again,

The fink – fate came into play,

Played the brutal chords,

That put an unassailable oasis,

Splitting the waters and the life

Making it lives.

Now, swans live on either side

Being parted and being hunted.

SOMEONE'S BLOOD
SOMEONE'S LOVE

It says, "Hi"

Making its presence

As I feel a kick within.

Finally, I am being blessed

After so much turmoil, and

Got something to cherish

Someone my own.

But, would it be alike

The gallant who lived me, or

The human who I share life with.

If the gallant resides in my womb,

I denounce its presence.

As, though, he will be mine

But I won't be his.

What if he is the human?

Would he capture someone's love?

In time to come, and

Pour his blood within.

Am I full or void?

As I beget someone's love

And someone's blood.

THE DAYS ARE BACK

Once the tapestry of fate

Enclosed the lives:

The two wandering souls

One being too lively

The other a little reserved

Nevertheless, both got entangled

In the frame of love.

Whereby, the needle of romance worked

Through the cloth of affection and care, and

Keep on making the two blank lives

More urging to live – for each other

As no one ever did for them.

Both felt complete

But, the masterpiece in making soon stopped

As if the God took a break

In blessing the fates, and

The needle of romance broke.

Somehow, the lively one was removed

And set into another frame

With an already complete life.

The pain last even longer than the split

As more aches smitten the reserved's existence

With the removal of the thread

Once wrapped around him

Making him feel complete.

It all happened

In the same breezes

In the same rains

In the same November.

Now, the days are back

Along with all its aching ruptures.

THE DAYS ARE NOT MINE

She pulls out the pin from hair

And the cataract fell,

Sits before her dressing table

To apply her night skin care treatment

As she is finished,

Gets to her bed

The bed, which once

I used to see

Through the camera online

Where she will roll over and over

Out of coyness

Making her chubby cheeks red

And dimples more ingrained.

Nevertheless, she just lies on her bed today

Not dreaming but

Disturbed with the thought –

Tomorrow's task of going university.

Once, it used to be her favourite part of the day

Musing over the sneaky glances to come

We would cast on each other

But now she repulses it

And just go to sleep

Tomorrow, she will get herself unwantedly

To the university

The sun will check on her

The classes will bore her

The sight of professors will ache her

No one will praise her eye – makeup

Nor the shade of lipstick she wore

Or the sandals giving comfort to my heaven

Surprisingly, she won't mind it

As she knows

It's over now

I am gone, and

The days are not mine

Ironically, it's the same moments and venues which you await to cash in for your well-being intend to decimate you.

LOOSER

Yes! She reads me today

But, with someone else's surname

She does meet me often,

Among the crowd,

Eager to catch me

Just as other fans.

She loves and lives me

Having my face in her Prince's eyes,

She groans, imagining

Ours body intact,

Unlikely to the truth.

She lives happily,

As promised to me

Pity, only the Prince get

To taste the spring.

I have everything

I aspired to achieve:

My famed carrier and Her

But, her not as mine

Rather, as no one

Just as many other goddesses,

Distant, forbidden and of someone else's.

LET'S MOVE ON

We are so biased when it comes to our sufferings. How could I claim so? Well, let me assure you all I am admittedly, absolutely, certainly and all the other adjectives which can embolden my conviction, right. Fate is a word unknown to us in normal course of life. We achieve something, oh, that is because of my determination and hard work I put it into my endeavour. Ok! You worked hard, didn't sleep proper for days and you got the reward. Fine enough. We are happy for you. The problem or the phenomenon of fate comes into play the moment a person gets enticed by some pretty eyes and waving hair or some can be charmed by even curly brown hair. Not an hour is passed, and the juveniles will thank their fate that made a bond of them. Each of the ten topics they discuss daily, one would be of the gratitude of having each other in their lives and the void life they lived till the romantic calamity occurred. Hours, days, weeks and months pass, and the event happen why I named the bonding a romantic calamity. Yes, the Romeo Juliet break up. You must notice that I didn't go beyond "months". I do know how to spell "year" and even know we can add "s" if there are more than "one." But the relation doesn't last to even singular of the "years." They fight. They curse. They hurt themselves. I get it, it sucks when someone you spend your precious time and eyesight part ways like there has been no one. Initially, only sobs and tears are in action.

Gradually, the target of curses shifts from the "beloved" to fate. Not only the patient himself but the circle around him also curse it. We all must have heard this out of the world statements "Come on, you need to move on. It was all in fate." This just doesn't end here. The patient curses his fate again and admits that the breakup was all in fate and says, "Let's move on." To be honest, all the Romeo and Juliets, read carefully. The fault is neither in stars nor in fate. The fault is in you. You need not to blame fate for your cringe. You need not to curse fate on behalf of your pathetic behaviour with one another. You need not to regret of having a fate like you have rather than accepting that it was you who were skeptic of one another's character. You just need to be honest with yourself, with your partner and with me as well.

The Confused Fate.

PAKISTAN'S WELL ESTABLISHED PUBLISHING HOUSE
TRUSTED BY LOCAL AND INTERNATIONAL AUTHORS

Done with writing your wonderful book ?

We will Publish It

Self Publishing and POD (Print On Demand) Made Easy

ISLAMABAD - PAKISTAN

www.auraqpublications.com.pk   @AuraqBooks
@AuraqPublications   +92 300 0571 530
Auraq Publications   Auraq Publications

www.ingramcontent.com/pod-product-compliance
Lightning Source LLC
Chambersburg PA
CBHW051428150726
48000CB00005B/1995